Echoes Of A Silent Heart

A Poetry Collection

Sahelipa Datta

BookLeaf Publishing

India | USA | UK

Made with ❤ on the BookLeaf Publishing Platform
www.bookleafpub.in
www.bookleafpub.com

Dedication

To all the quiet souls whose journeys are marked by both silence and strength.

To every heart that has ever whispered a prayer, shed a tear, or quietly believed in hope.

For those who continue to find beauty in the unspoken and courage in their own story.

This is for you.

This book is for the brave ones who face life's trials with resilience, finding beauty in moments of stillness and grace in the darkest of times. May you find comfort in these words, for they are a reflection of the path we all share—a journey of healing, hope, and self-discovery.

To my heart, my inspiration, and the countless stories waiting to be told in silence.

Preface

"Echoes of a Silent Heart" is a journey through the quiet, unspoken corners of the soul. Each poem is a reflection of the emotions, thoughts, and experiences that often go unnoticed in the noise of everyday life.

This collection captures the delicate dance between silence and expression, where the heart resonates within each line, where words echo the deepest of feelings— love, loss, hope, and healing.

I invite you to explore the gentle rhythms and whispers within these pages, where every line is a reminder that even in silence, there is a story waiting to be told.

Acknowledgements

I am deeply grateful to my parents for their endless support and belief in me throughout this entire process.

My sincere thanks go to my sister, who helped me regain my confidence every time I felt hopeless.

I am deeply grateful to my close-knit circle of brothers, sisters, and friends, whose constant encouragement was a source of strength whenever I needed it.

A special thank you to my school and college for nurturing and shaping me in the way I am today.

I would also like to extend my heartfelt appreciation to BookLeaf Publishing for giving me the platform to express my thoughts and words on such a grand scale.

Lastly, I offer my sincere thanks to each of you holding this book. Your continued cooperation and support inspire me to publish more of my work in the future.

I welcome your reviews and thoughts — feel free to share them with me via email at dattasahelipa08@gmail.com

1. Illusion

Illusion...
Can sometimes be a healer,
Can also act as a killer.

    Can save life from fading,
    Can halt you from shredding.

Can be true, can be fake,
Can spark a bold outbreak.

    Can often turn into a guide,
    Can also wound your pride.

Can give you bright lights,
Can even cast eclipse sights.

    Can make you skeptical,
    Can build a deceptive wall.

Can be a lamp, a guide in the dark,
Can catch fire and go berserk.

Illusion...
The one you trust too much,

Can bear an illusive touch;
Illusion can come without a clue—
Illusion can be people too!

2. Friend or Foe?

Friend or foe? That's yours to decide,
But take time, let truth be your guide.
Friend to foe? Too easy a change,
Foe to friend? Now that sounds strange!

A foe can wear a friendly guise,
With practiced words and hollow ties.
But you are strong, your heart is wise—
Never trust too soon; think twice.

Ever you face a darkened eve,
When shadows whisper, hearts deceive...
The truth will cut— no time to grieve—
In a second, they will leave.

3. Wings of Change

The gentle green, breathing deep,
Peeking shyly from an oak leaf.

Leaving a shadow, prettily curled,
Eager to know a whole new world.

Then comes the change, growing alone,
From a caterpillar to one fully grown.

The whispers of nature, the secrets of tide,
Carrying onward, embracing the ride.

Depicting the beauty in life's grand rise,
Its ways to wander, to dream, to strive.

With colors that travel, stir, and evoke,
Blending like an artist's brushstrokes.

Its delicate wings, in graceful flight,
Turning the dark into morning light.

Dipped in sunset, kissed by rain,
Painting the world again and again.

And in this dance, so wild and free,
The butterfly hums a melody.

4. Being You

"They"—there, they'll tittle-tattle...
Oh, maybe they'll judge...
Why shed tears for that?
Why worry so much?

Your eyes dream for you—
Hearty, hefty, high...
Your goals, your dreams—
You must reify.

Just embrace that one act—
The one making you keen.
Even if you lose throughout,
Trust me, you will win.

5. Nature's Way

Nature provides a new way to live...
Nature teaches a new way to forgive.

Nature uplifts you when you feel low...
Nature shows the path to help you grow.

Nature's rhythm flows in river streams,
Nature fills your heart, Nature fuels your dreams.

Nature brings light to your darkness...
Nature gives hope in times of stress.

Nature holds your pain without a sound,
Nature lifts your soul from off the ground.

Nature feels you—and your inside...
Nature is so colourful, though it's green outside.

6. Ashes

A lifeless beginning, a silent despair,
Warnings from life hung thick in the air.
Yet no one listened, no soul was prepared—
The truth stood tall, but no heart dared.

Life trudged on, in struggle and strife,
Bare to the bone, the core of its life.
Yet voices arose, cold whispers and lies,
Calling it folly, a grand disguise.

Still life fought, in frost and in flame,
Chasing a goal, nameless, no name.
It ran through storms, through joy and disgrace—
Till it turned to ashes, lost in the race.

7. The Beauty and The Beast

Mysterious, the ground...
Mystery in the sky...
Mysteriously I found,
Two little butterflies.

They played in the leaves,
Danced through the air,
Bound by true beliefs,
A vision rare and fair.

I stood there still,
With a cup of tea,
Drinking in the thrill
Of Nature's harmony.

I whispered to me,
"Oh! What a scene..."
And longed to be
Part of that dream.

I tried to freeze,
That perfect hue,
But time, like breeze,
Let moments through.

Then shadows came,
Swift as a gust...
Their joy to maim,
And turn to dust.

Unaware they lay,
In blissful delight,
While danger made way
From shadows in flight.

I wished to run,
To break through snow,
To scream at the sun,
To shield them below.

But before my stride—
Could bridge the flame,
The moment had died—
I had lost the game.

They fluttered and fled,
Scattered in fear,
But silence spread...
No cry reached ear.

In golden decay,

Of the sun's last plea,
One became the prey,
One—lucky escapee.

And as I stood,
Beneath that tree,
It felt like childhood
Returning to me...

Where dreams would appear,
Then slowly decay—
As Beauty shone clear,
Till the Beast stole the day.

8. Quarantined souls

It was a normal, drifting day...
Two months still to welcome May.
Returned to my quiet space,
Like always—with a tired face.

Letting my energy slip away,
Bracing again for the next day.
Beneath the moon's soft silver tune,
I met my bed—perhaps too soon.

Who knew, just suddenly,
The world would change so endlessly?
News would echo, fast and loud,
And every hope wear a dark shroud.

Weekdays melted into one,
As if the race of time was done.
Families drawn near once more,
While hidden talents found a door.

A stream of silence gushed throughout,
While the world's noise burned out.
As if Nature, with suppressed cries,
Brought her fury from the skies.

As though all creatures took their stand,
Whispering justice, hand in hand.
And in one voice, they firmly spat—
"We've had enough—Tit for Tat."

Who ever dreamt a tiny strain,
Could bring the mighty world such pain?
Who knew, post tales of *Ramayana*,
We'd script a war called *Corona*?

Now the world walks through the night,
Ashamed to bear the morning light.
In the cloak of haunting haze,
All our paths became a maze.

Days arrived we couldn't greet,
Grief and fear in every street.
Trembling in this poisoned air,
Hope grew thin—yet lingered there.

A mother longs to touch her child,
But boundaries have turned us wild.
Caged in walls, minds confined,
Life itself—quarantined.

Still, some embers brightly glow,

A belief that soon we'll break this flow.
This chain, this curse, this endless ring—
Won't outlive what courage can bring.

Yes, we'll rise and fiercely fight,
Reclaim the day, embrace the night.
We'll gear again, and bravely strive,
To breathe anew... to feel alive.

But what of the virus deep inside,
That fear has birthed and egos hide?
It haunts the mind, feeds on dismay,
Whispers darkness every day.

And questions now the soul must weigh—
Can truth still find its way?
Is this a game of silent war,
Or a wound we carved—and let it scar?

9. Cycles of us

I have seen them blaming the Sun,
When the scorching heat has just begun...
Then begging again for a touch of its light,
When the streets freeze over, cold as night.

I have seen the wealthy cry and pray,
Asking God for more each day...
While some just wait with empty hands,
Hoping for charity in barren lands.

I have seen crimes without a care,
No fear, no guilt, just cold despair...
Then pleading for forgiveness deep,
When no solution lies to reap.

I have seen the floods arise,
Hungry hearts beneath grey skies...
Then watched them taint the soil and air,
When gentle breezes danced with care.

I have seen the cruel drought unfold,
A silent plea for water bold...
Then careless wastage floods the street,
Where once they cried for just a beat.

I have seen changing reveries,
Turning into insomnia's miseries...
Again seen those become a nightmare,
Born of phobia and deep despair.

10. VIBGYOR

The festival of colours,
The chromatic Holi,
A bouquet of smiles and success—
From me to you, wholly.

    There is something,
    Something higher than view,
    Awareness and deep spirituality—
    Like the colour Violet, are rare and few.

Wisdom and justice,
May they always guide you,
With integrity and sincerity—
Like the colour Indigo, pure and true.

    Serene and peaceful,
    Let calmness flow through,
    With poise and responsibility—
    Like the colour Blue, so few.

Nature is our mother,
Let reverence bloom in you,
With grace and gentle tranquility—
Like the colour Green, calm in hue.

Joyful and artistic,
Let bright hopes renew,
With radiant optimism—
Like the colour Yellow, shining through.

Sunlit and spirited,
Let courage carry you,
With passion and fierce creativity—
Like the colour Orange, bold and true.

Loving and daring,
Let your heart pursue
Goodness and fearless bravery—
Like the colour Red, just a few.

All the colours in this world,
Bring joy and meaning new—
In the sky, they shine as rainbows,
On the earth, they shine through you.

11. Done and Dusted

It's okay if you feel low,
Today, let the soft tears flow;
Soon, the "strong" within you'll meet,
Smiling in the mirror — calm and sweet.

You're not weak — you never were,
Strength like yours will always stir.
Dream the highest, chase the light,
You're your saviour, day and night.

You've achieved so much already,
With a heart so brave and steady.
Your willpower, your patience true,
Together build the best of you.

To your torn life, hope is thread,
Stitching light where fear once bled.
No matter how the world's adjusted,
You'll rise and leave it *Done and Dusted*.

12. Dreams

Dreams?
Dreams are those that let you live,
Dreams are those that let you think deep.

Dreams are those that let you reign,
Dreams are those that keep you keen.

Dreams are those that let you be brisk,
Dreams are those that let you take risk.

Dreams are those that sense your price,
Dreams are those that help you act wise.

So, let them flow throughout the soul;
Fill them with love, hug with your whole.
They don't have wings, can't waft in the sky;
But they have the power to make you happy and fly.

To sum up, they can be tough;
On the dot, you can't address enough.
Yet you can define them easily,
In your way, proper and matchlessly.

Dreams?

From reverie, do make them insomnia;
But forget as nightmare, if ever turns phobia.

13. In the Sky

Mild winds whisper from above,
Red clouds drift like dreams of love.
I stand here, close to the sky,
Lost in a view that stuns the eye.

Amidst this vast and endless blue,
Magical jets go soaring through.
Soft music plays, the night feels light,
As bats take flight in quiet delight.

A sudden spark of yellow gleams,
Like winter bells in frosted dreams.
I felt that pleasing luminosity,
Might paint a new fairytale in the city.

14. The Day, You

The day your faith was shaken,
The day your spirit was broken,
The day you lost trust on self,
The day your mind cried out for help,
The day your powers crumbled,
The day your heart secretly rattled/trembled,
The day you off tracked/ derailed all energies,
The day you couldn't find happy keys,
The day you saw failure all-around,
The day your tears touched the ground;

That day, did you stop by?
Did you pause to think/wonder 'why'?
That day, did you truly cry?
That day, did you disbelieve "I"?

But if that darkness never arrived,
You would have never valued light!
If that despair did never ignite,
You would have never learned to fight!

And if that horror never crashed your inside,
Would you have ever achieved your today's height?

15. Red

Red...

Does it only scream "beware"?
Only wrath in a stranger's stare?
Does it always mean to fight,
A flashing sign, a burning light?

But how can you so soon forget—
The love, the roses, the sunset?
A billion blooms, a blushing hue,
That speaks of hearts forever true.

Yes! That very shade, vermilion,
That blooms with grace—a soft rebellion.
Not just of rage or warning said,
But of passion, warmth—
                    The soul of Red.

16. The Mirror

Today I woke up...
In front of a giant mirror,
Smiling at me, it asked—
"Command me anything, dear Master..."

"You know I'm the king
Of this grand empire—
Bring me the powers of the world,
All happiness, here and now, entire!"

The mirror spoke, "Forgive me, sir...
What you ask is far too steep.
The only way to afford such wealth—
Is to have a soul pure and deep."

"And you think I'm impure?
Look closer—your faults aren't new.
If I'm a devil in heart and soul,
Your morals are questionable too."

"I agree, Master, truly...
For your choices shape me too.
How could I ever hope to grow
Different from what you do?"

"Your attitude is too mean,
You're no hero, no star.
And I can't grant a thing to you—
Not even a wish from afar."

A quiet silence fell around...
"I'm sorry, my friend.
I realize now where I went wrong,
And I promise, myself I'll mend."

"You are my eternal image—
I'll nourish you with care.
Your strength, your light, your truth—
Together, we'll repair."

"I knew you would one day
Unveil your truest light.
And we'll relive the joy again—
Where lies don't blur the sight."

"Today you've learned,
The finest lesson, my king—
That friendship gains everything...
And enmity gains nothing."

17. Chasing Shadows

I kept choosing night over day,
Wishing its calm would forever stay.
Each dawn, I staged a stubborn fight—
To hold the dark, resist the light.

I set each evening like a game,
A match I played, yet lost the same.
Each catch I missed, each chance slipped by,
Beneath the ever-changing sky.

Frustrated, I cried out in spite,
"Who gave you such a daring right?
Why can't you stay and never stray?
I'm tired of goodbye every day."

Just then, two eyes as soft as shade,
In moonlit laughter, gently played.
They teased me with a quiet grace,
A calm that time could not erase.

"If I remained and ceased to flee,
Tell me, how bright would morning be?
If darkness clung and blocked the way,
How would you ever welcome day?"

18. A Day Unlike Before

Today the sun refused to shine,
Today no insect dared to whine,
Today the clouds held back their rain,
Today I felt no trace of pain.

Today, nature seemed so strange,
As if it longed for some great change,
As if it wept in soft defeat,
And yearned to find a brand-new beat.

My eagerness was so extreme—
I couldn't let it lose its gleam!
I tried to catch it, raw, uncut,
And begged the world to not disrupt.

I trembled, wondering within,
Would anyone just listen in?
A sudden flash, a golden beam—
Revealed to me: it was a dream.

And now, all things seem vague, unclear,
I found those thoughts so hard to bear.
Then came a whisper, calm and near:
It said, *"Never, ever hold on to fear."*

19. Chains

Children, like flowers, so pure and bright,
Innocent souls glowing with light.
Their wishes are small, yet dreams run deep,
In their little hearts, big hopes they keep.

They dream with laughter, in silent ways,
Imagining worlds where magic stays.
A universe built from joy and art,
With wonder blooming in every heart.

But what of you—your cruel deeds?
Your selfish ways, your heart that bleeds,
Not love, but harshness, cold and vain—
What is it, truly, you hope to gain?

They are kind, they trust with grace,
They live with morals, in every place.
So don't pretend with pity's guise,
While truth is hidden behind your lies.

They can't protest, they're not that strong,
So they obey, not knowing wrong.
You preach to them: "Stand on your own,"
Yet strip their rights, to build your throne.

The smile you wear—so false, so sly,
Breeds hopes in them, but it's a lie.
With food and coins, you play your game,
Turning their lives into halls of shame.

Look at their faces, quiet, worn—
Each silent glance, a soul that's torn.
Try to listen, try to feel,
And maybe your heart will start to heal.

Look in their eyes, and you will see,
A world of pain and misery.
Your deeds, have dimmed their light—
This is the truth, this is their fight.

You call yourself a hero, bold—
Yet steal their futures, dreams left cold.
In truth, you're earning just disgrace,
A zero carved upon your face.

Don't shatter childhood with your greed,
They have bright minds the world will need.
They're not your servants, nor your toy,
They're children, full of life and joy.

They have a right—to learn, to play,

To shape tomorrow, to lead the way.
Stop clouding their futures with your clay,
Let them rise into the day.

Remember this—no wrong goes free,
Karma watches silently.
The lesson's harsh when justice comes,
And you will hear those beating drums.

So be the change, the light, the guide,
Stand with them, not in pride.
For if you don't, the day will rise—
When they'll look back with fearless eyes.

And then you'll face the truth, once veiled—
The voices you silenced... now loudly hailed.

20. Lost in the Abyss

One winter morning,
Walking down the lane,
All alone in solitude,
With freedom—not like the insane.

Winds were blowing mild,
Leaves rustled soft and light,
The sky a blend of blue and white,
The air and sun both gentle, bright.

But after walking miles ahead,
The light was gone, replaced by dread.
The sky turned black without a clue,
And I had lost the path I knew.

Darkness closed from all around,
I found myself beneath the ground—
Not trapped like a prisoner in chain,
Yet far from tales of Arabian fame.

You know that Genie, in the golden light?
With Aladdin, our childhood knight?
The hero we praised, brave and adored—
But here, no magic, no sword is stored.

My mind was clouded, filled with stress,
How do I escape this mess?
Should I slay the demon here,
And reshape the world without fear?

The sides were scary, bones and stones,
Skulls and pebbles, chilling moans.
Horrors danced before my eyes,
Silent screams replaced my cries.

What to do? Where to turn?
Whom to trust? Whom to spurn?
Should I hope for help to come,
Or face it alone—undone, undone?

No answers came; no guiding light.
I stood alone within the night.
I failed, I wept—I gave it up,
The poison deep within my cup.

And then I wondered, who's to blame?
The deity? The world? This wretched game?

CUTTTT...
To my surprise—what did I hear?
A loud voice echoed, bright and clear:

"Great shot, now let's shoot—
'The Shutter'— on pursuit!"

Laughter rose, sweets were passed,
Moment shifted, free at last.

Again it started— what a passion:
"Lights! Camera! And... Action!"

21. Look Back

Sun shines...

I'm... I'm so happy...
My heart can barely stay—
He's finally coming home...
After two whole years away.

Done with his MBA,
He's coming back at last.
I've counted every second,
Each moment from the past.

I've waited here in silence,
By the window, all alone...
Eyes fixed on that old lane,
Wishing he'd just phone.

Tears would come uninvited,
But I'd wipe them every time—
Holding onto memories
Like verses in a rhyme.

Today! Oh, today!
I'll welcome him with pride.

And I'll wrap him in my arms,
There's joy I cannot hide.

I still recall those days—
Teaching him to walk,
Guiding tiny trembling steps,
Showing him how to talk.

From counting 0 to 9,
And saying A, B, C...
He learned so fast,
It always amazed me.

I smile without knowing,
Reliving those golden days.
Though they're long gone,
In my heart, their memory stays.

Then—suddenly, a sound...
The doorbell starts to ring.
My heart skips a beat—
Is this the joy it will bring?

I open it quickly—
And there he stands.
But... someone is with him,
Holding onto his hands.

I welcome them inside,
Still lost in tender grace...
But questions fill my chest
As I search his face.

"Mom, meet my wife," he says.
"It's been two months, you see..."
Two months? And not a word?
You didn't tell me? Me?

"Oh Mom," he says, smiling,
"I wanted you to cheer.
I thought this happy news
Would bring you joy, not tear."

I nod and force a smile,
Though silence hugs my chest.
Something feels so different...
A twist I never guessed.

From that day on,
He barely met my gaze...
The bond we had was fading—
Lost in busy days.

I watched their laughter bloom,

Felt my presence start to blur.
In their perfect little world,
There was no place for her...

The woman who once held him,
Through fevers, fears, and fall—
Now sat like a stranger,
Unnoticed in the hall.

Sun shines again...

But clouds begin to creep.
Even the warmest rays
Can't wake what lies too deep.

Never did I dream
That love would come to this—
A lifetime of sacrifice,
Rewarded with a miss.

"Mom, we'll settle abroad,
We're moving to Rome.
Would you prefer a maid,
Or an old-age home?"

My eyes blurred over,
My voice held a smile—

"I'll manage, don't you worry—
You go and live in style."

They left, hand in hand,
He didn't turn around.
And silence moved in slowly,
Without a single sound.

Alone again, completely—
Perhaps this is my fate.
But I'm not angry, no…
Just quietly desolate.

I never had imagined
That dreams could end this way—
With empty hands and aching heart
And nothing left to say.

But he is happy now,
His life is shining bright…
And maybe that's enough
To sleep alone at night.

A mother gives, and gives, and gives,
Till nothing's left to lack—
I sit here still, wondering—
Will he ever *look back*?

22. If I Could...

Sometimes I truly wish...
I could become invisible—
To face the world from shadows,
And be alone, yet stable.

I'd roam across the cities,
Sit anywhere I please,
With a magic wand in hand,
And chants that ride the breeze.

To see true colours surface,
While I watch in silent grace,
To stop a crime with just my fear,
A ghost in time and space.

To end the pain around me,
The torture and the cries,
To stop the acid's evil burn,
And silence all the lies.

Erase the lines of faith and caste,
That rip the world apart,
And stitch it back together
With threads of healing heart.

No rumors and no terror,
No jealousy, no fights—
Just Mother Nature smiling,
Bathed in gentle lights.

To bring the pure days back again,
To spark the world with powers,
To rebuild all the innocence,
And gift back laughing hours.

To break the wrong decisions,
To guide with truth and steer,
To give the crying child a voice,
And wipe away each fear.

I'd erase all discrimination,
Each hateful, toxic trait—
Surprise the world with wonders,
And cleanse the soul from hate.

But deep within, I know the truth—
These dreams may never be,
A reverie that flickers,
In harsh reality.

Yet even if I can't be ghost,

Or wield a mystic rod,
One spark remains within me—
The purest gift from God:

To make each heart a newborn child,
So love and truth can grow,
Where only morals shine through bright,
And wild thoughts never show.

23. Today

Today, let your smile softly bloom,
Chase away shadows, clear every gloom.
Let troubles return to the restless shore,
And weigh on your spirit nevermore.

Today, take a breath—so calm, so deep,
Let go of the worries, you no longer keep.
In your heart, let boldness rise,
In your mind, let starlight fill the skies.

Today, awaken your hidden might,
Make golden use of morning's light.
Believe in the balance, trust the scale,
Let blooming hope and joy prevail.

Today, your dreams may feel afar,
Like whispers lost in a wandering star.
But within you burns that sacred fire—
A soul alight with pure desire.

So walk with grace, just as you are—
For deep within, you are a star.

24. The Girl

The girl with an innocent smile,
Winning hearts without a trace of guile.
Unmoved by pampering or praise,
Her words, once spoken, set ablaze.
A joyful laugh she'd freely share,
Hand in hand with her mother there.
With eyes that shone and curls that swirled,
She offered glimpses of a perfect world.

Once in a while, she'd quietly cry,
Yet still shone gentle as the sky.
Her giggles danced in sweet refrain,
A melody replayed again and again.

Then came the night—so cruel, so cold,
A tale too tragic, too dark to be told.
The world came crashing before her gaze,
She stood there stunned, lost in a haze.
Strangers loomed with shadows unknown,
She whispered, broken, "Why was I born?"

No gold, no joy, no hidden treasure,
Just stolen dreams and vanished pleasure.
Fear consumed her soul and mind,

No safety, no haven left to find.

Where was the smile, once pure and wide?
Where was the laughter she'd never hide?
Now on the road, she lay and bled,
The world around her—red, so red.

To a hospital, shattered, she was brought,
While prayers rose high with every thought.
The crowd cast stones instead of grace,
While her mother clung with a tear-stained face.

Then silence came... the final breath,
Her tender soul embraced by death.
All the hopes, all dreams undone,
Decorated now, but forever gone.

No longer haunted by fearful cries,
She rests beneath the endless skies.
She never strayed, not led astray—
Could she have known life would betray?

Yes, it differed—a little bit...
But still they judged and never quit.
Yet through the silence, her whisper flies:
"I wished to live, dear mother... to rise."

25. The Language of Light

They slip through cracks as night is torn,
Gold threads of hush that welcome morn.
They stitch the silence into song—
A breath of hope where hearts belong.

They cradle leaves in softest grace,
Touch sleeping buds, then light the space.
They brush the shadows of each tree—
A gentle guide for eyes to see.

But tender beams begin to burn,
As noon arrives and moments turn.
They etch the truth on skin and land—
A fire too fierce for some to stand.

They shape the world, they keep the signs,
Fade old stories, blur the lines.
What once was vivid turns to pale—
A memory caught in sunlight's trail.

They peel the soul, lay bare the bone,
Reveal the heart when most alone.
No shade to hide, no cloak to wear—
Just truths too fierce for souls to bear.

Yet still we chase them through the flame,
Though every step may end in blame.
For even, as the bright winds bite,
They hold the thread that leads to light.

So let them bless when noon is done,
Let them mark both curse and sun.
For in the language of their blaze,
Lives every truth the soul obeys.

9 789370 924598